LITTLE KIDS FIRST BIG BOOK OF WHY

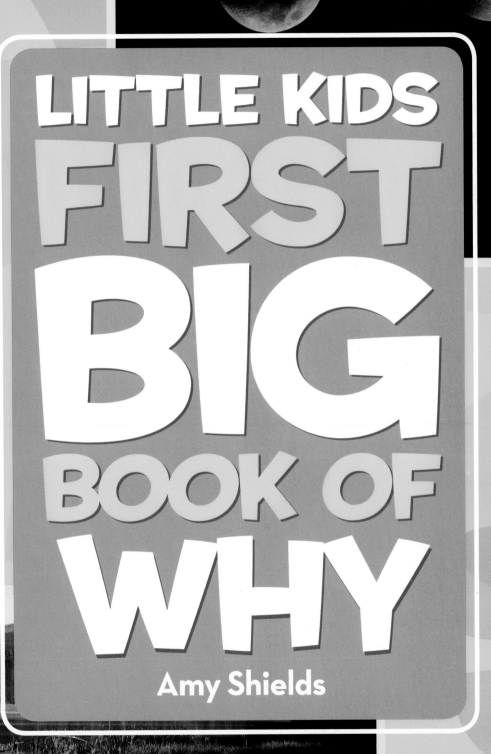

LITTLE KIDS
FIRST
BIG
BOOK OF
WHY

Amy Shields

NATIONAL GEOGRAPHIC KiDS

WASHINGTON, D.C.

CONTENTS

Why does Grandma have **WRINKLES?**

Why do I have **CURLY HAIR?**

6

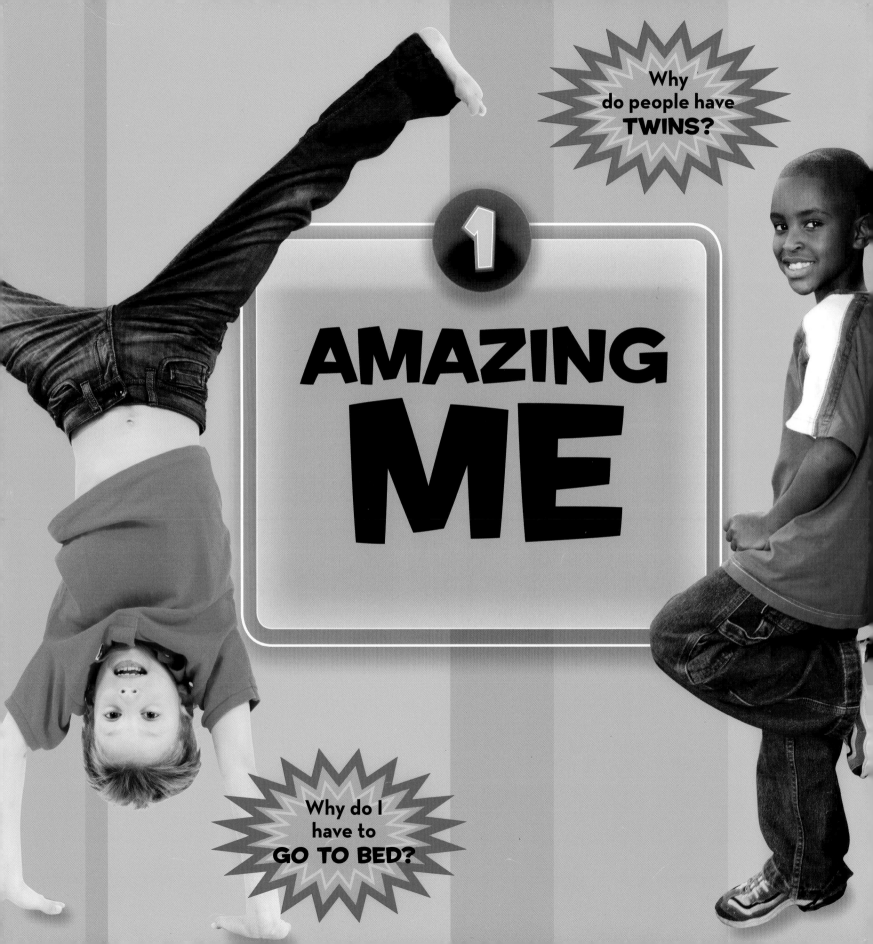

1

AMAZING
ME

Why
do people have
TWINS?

Why do I
have to
GO TO BED?

WHY AM I SPECIAL?

You are a one and only!
There is nobody else in the world exactly like you. Even identical twins are different in some ways.

Your outside is way different from your inside. The skin, hair, and nails on the outside of your body are not alive. But inside… there's a party going on!

Just hours after birth, you knew your mother by **HER SMELL.**

Nobody else has **eyes** exactly like yours. Your **fingerprints**, footprints, and tongue print are not like anybody else's.

FACTS

KIND OF ANIMAL
Mammal

SPECIES
Homo sapiens, which means "wise human"

HOME
Every livable place on Earth

SIZE
Average males in the U.S. grow to 5'9" (1.75 meters), and females are slightly smaller

FOOD
Omnivorous

SOUNDS
6,909 languages

HOW MANY BABIES?
Usually one, up to eight at a time

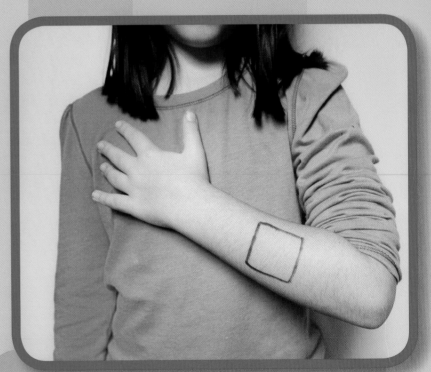

DRAW A 1-BY-1-INCH BOX ON YOUR ARM.

That skin space contains: 3 yards (2.7 meters) of blood vessels, 4 yards (3.5 meters) of nerve fibers, 1,300 nerve cells, 100 sweat glands, 3 million cells, 32 million bacteria. Imagine what's going on in the rest of your body!

9

WHY ARE PEOPLE DIFFERENT COLORS?

All skin colors come from melanin. Your body makes melanin to protect your skin from burning in the sun. Kids whose ancestors came from sunny places are born with more melanin, and **darker skin.** Kids whose ancestors came from less sunny places are born with less melanin, and **lighter skin.**

10

Freckles are clumps of **MELANIN.**

Put a **Band-Aid** around your finger on a sunny day. **Take it off a few days later.** Did your body make any **melanin?** No! The Band-Aid blocked the sun from the skin. When sunlight hits your skin, melanin comes to shade it, giving you a **tan.**

11

WHY DO I HAVE A BELLY BUTTON?

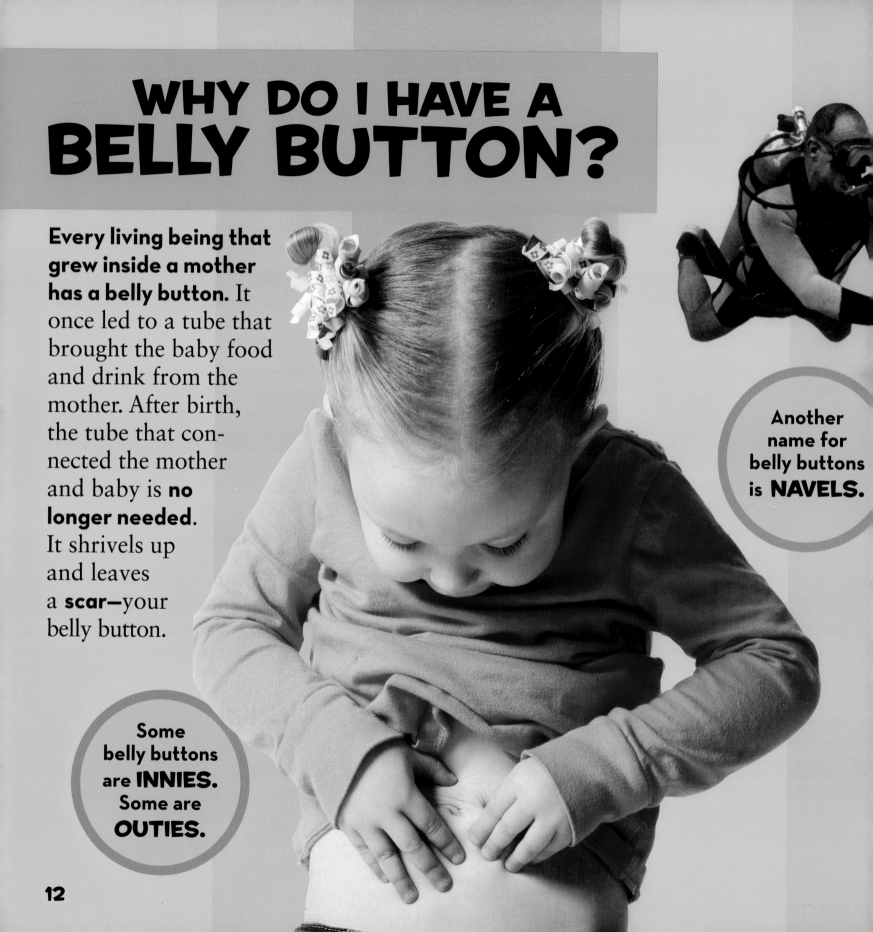

Every living being that grew inside a mother has a belly button. It once led to a tube that brought the baby food and drink from the mother. After birth, the tube that connected the mother and baby is **no longer needed**. It shrivels up and leaves a **scar**—your belly button.

Another name for belly buttons is **NAVELS.**

Some belly buttons are **INNIES.** Some are **OUTIES.**

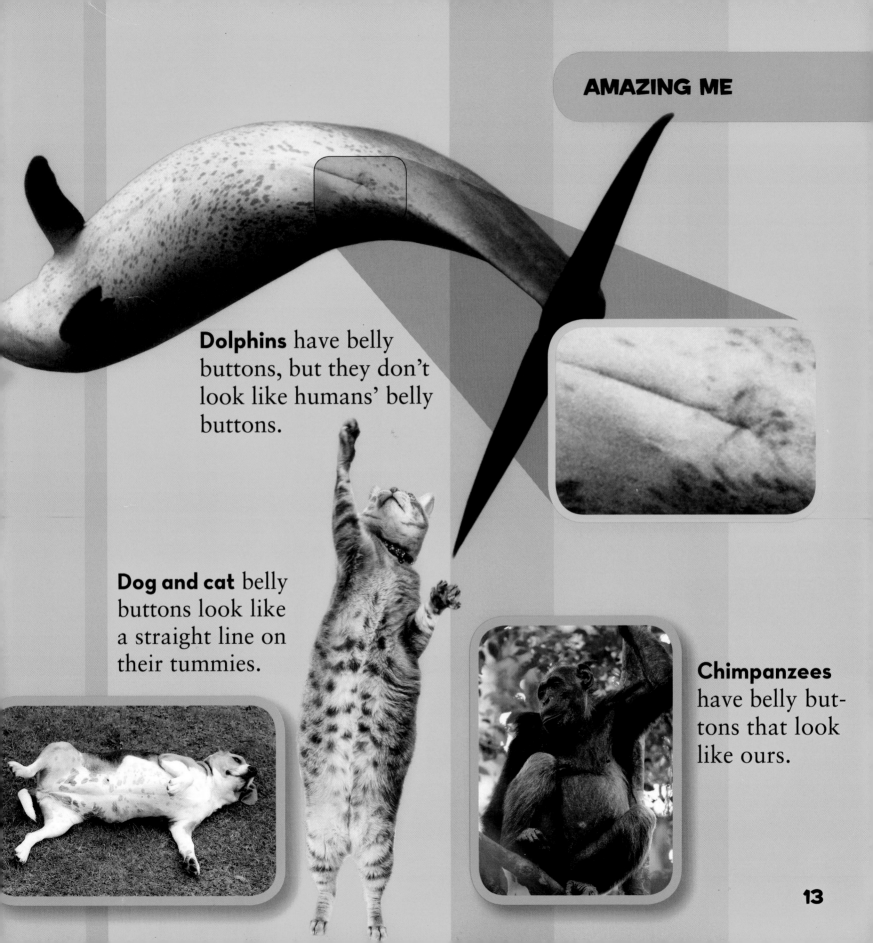

Dolphins have belly buttons, but they don't look like humans' belly buttons.

Dog and cat belly buttons look like a straight line on their tummies.

Chimpanzees have belly buttons that look like ours.

13

WHY DO SOME PEOPLE HAVE TWINS?

Human moms usually don't give birth to more than one baby at a time. **Humans have identical twins purely by chance.** Twins who are identical are made from one egg that splits. Fraternal twins, who look different, are made from two eggs.

Three babies from one mom are called **TRIPLETS.** Four are called **QUADRUPLETS.**

Identical twins are born almost exactly alike. But they may dress or cut their hair differently. You can always tell twins apart if you know them well.

RECIPE FOR A FAMILY EXPERIMENT

You are a mix of your mom and dad, with a little bit of nature and chance mixed in. How are you like your family? How are you different?

HE CAN!

NOT SO MUCH.

SHE CAN!

1 Look at Mom, Dad, sisters, brothers, aunts, uncles, cousins, and grandparents....

2 Look at hair. Who has curly hair? Who has straight hair? Who has a clockwise hair whorl?

3 Look at tongue twisting. Can anyone make a tongue curl?

4 Does anyone share the same nose shape? A dimple? Eye color? You and your family share so much. But there is only one you!

WHY DOES MY SKIN WRINKLE IN THE TUB?

When you put your hands or feet in warm water, your body tells the blood vessels in your fingers and toes to get smaller. This leaves spaces in your finger. Your skin sucks in to fill these spaces, and that gives you wrinkles! **The wrinkles on your fingertips help you grip things when you're wet, and the wrinkles on your toes make you less slippery when you get out of the tub.**

Did you know?
Your skin is flaking off all the time. You get a whole new layer of skin about once a month!

The thinnest skin on your body is your **EYELIDS.**

? The skin on the palms of your hands and soles of your feet is **EXTRA THICK.** Can you think why?

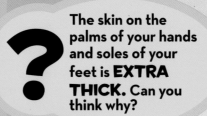

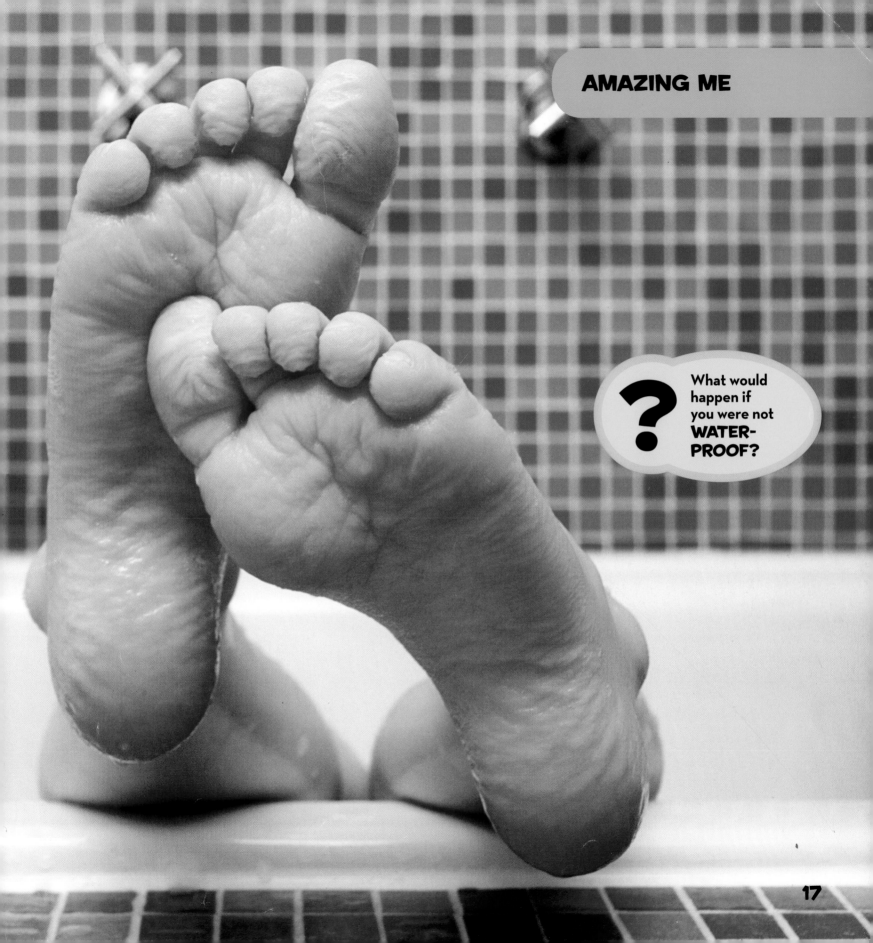

? What would happen if you were not **WATER-PROOF?**

WHY DOES GRANDMA HAVE WRINKLES?

Skin grows and stretches as you grow from baby size to adult. When you've been an adult for a while, skin stops growing and stretching. **It gets a little tired and a little less elastic.**

The lines you make when you smile today are where your wrinkles will be when you are old. A lifetime of laughter helps your skin wrinkle very nicely.

Laugh lines on the sides of eyes are called **CROW'S FEET.**

Pinch the skin on the back of your hand and see how fast it bounces back into place. Then find the oldest person you know and gently pinch the skin on the back of his or her hand. What happens?

This dog is called a Shar-Pei.
Unlike people, these dogs start out wrinkly as puppies and grow smoother as grown-up dogs.

19

WHY DOES THE DOCTOR LOOK IN MY THROAT?

Doctors use their senses to help people. They look, listen, and touch. A healthy throat is pink and wet. Red splotches, white dots, swollen tonsils, or an infected **uvula** (that little dangly thing) are all signs that can tell a doctor if you are sick.

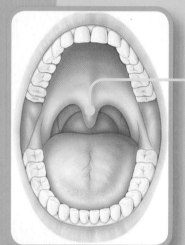

? What does a **UVULA** do? Some doctors don't think it does anything. What do you think of that?

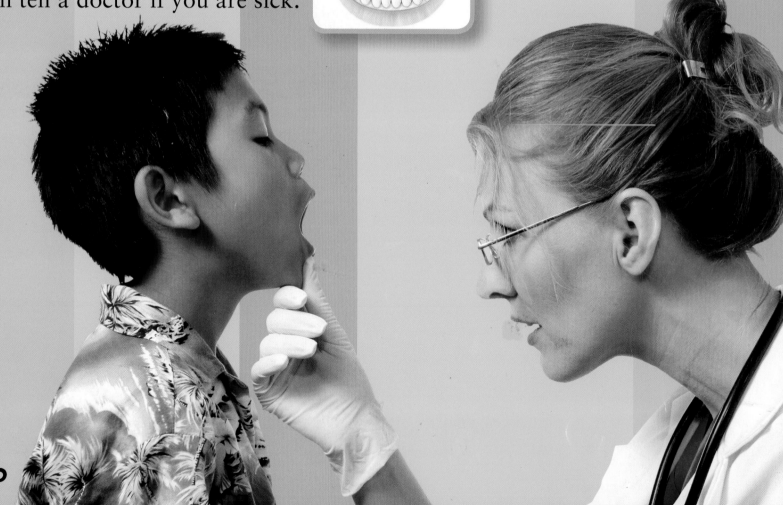

LISTEN-IN EXPERIMENT

Listening to your body is a way of making sure it's working right.

YOU'LL NEED

1- to 2-foot (30–60 centimeter) length of plastic tubing

2 funnels

Doctors say a beating **HEART SOUNDS** like *lub-dub*. What do you think?

1 Place the funnels in each end of the tubing. If it's a tight fit, heat the ends of the tubing with a hair dryer to make it stretch.

2 Put one funnel to your ear and the other over your heart, just above your left breast.

3 Do 20 jumping jacks and listen again. How is it different?

4 Try listening to your stomach. Does it sound different before you eat and after you eat?

21

WHY DO BABY TEETH FALL OUT?

If you did not have any teeth you'd still be eating mushy baby food. Kids need teeth to eat, but there is only room for 20 kid-size teeth in your kid-size mouth. As you grow, these **teeth get pushed out** as your bigger grown-up teeth grow in. Grown-ups have 32 big teeth. These teeth need to last a lifetime.

FACTS

MOST UNUSUAL TOOTH
The Narwhal's

BIGGEST TEETH
Elephant tusks

MOST COLORFUL
Beaver teeth are orange

SHARPEST TEETH
The red-bellied piranha's

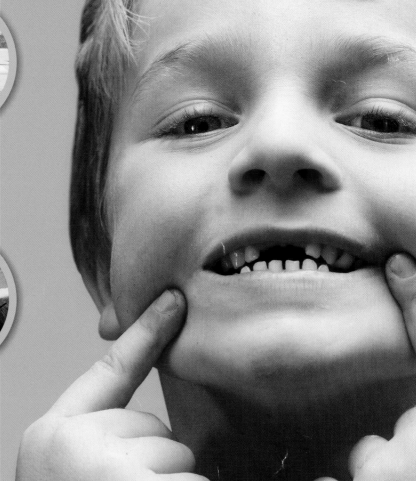

The first toothbrush was a **STICK WITH A MASHED END** to rub teeth clean.

BACTERIA (back-TEER-ree-ah) are alive. They live everywhere on Earth, and inside every living thing.

WHY DO I HAVE TO BRUSH MY TEETH?

When you eat, food gets left on your teeth. **The food you eat is also food for bacteria.** The bacteria can eat holes in your teeth if you don't brush them off and wash them away.

Crocodiles can grow as many as **3,000 TEETH** in a lifetime.

If you eat too many **CARROTS** your skin might turn orange.

Brushing your teeth and taking a bath clean your outside. **Eating vegetables cleans your inside.**

WHY DO I HAVE TO EAT VEGETABLES?

Vegetables have fiber. **Fiber** is like a scrub brush in your body.

Vegetables also have vitamins. Bodies need vitamins to grow and stay healthy.

Most sugar comes from two plants— **SUGARCANE** and **SUGAR BEETS.**

Candy tastes good. When humans like the taste of something, we eat it.

WHY DO I LIKE CANDY?

NO SWEET FRUIT IS POISON. Humans learned that sweet things were OK to eat.

Long, long, long, LONG ago, fruit was one of the only sweet treats. Fruit is good for you. The sugar in fruit gives you energy and makes it taste good. We learned to like sweet things.

25

WHY DO I HAVE CURLY HAIR?

Hair grows through tiny strawlike tubes that are in your skin. These tubes are called **follicles**. Follicles can be different shapes.
Some are round.
Some are oval.
Some are almost flat.

Our heads have over **100,000** follicles.

Thick hair means you have bigger follicles, not more.

? Do your parents have **CURLY HAIR?** Chances are if their hair is curly, yours is too.

Flat follicles make **CURLY HAIR.**

Oval follicles make **WAVY HAIR.**

Eyelashes are a different kind of hair.

The palms of your **HANDS** and the bottom of your **FEET** have no follicles, and no hair.

Round follicles make **STRAIGHT HAIR.**

27

You might **think** it hurts, but it doesn't. Break a little bit off the bottom of one of your head hairs. **It doesn't hurt because it's not alive.**

Now give a sharp, fast pull to one of your head hairs. **Ouch! Your hair is alive under the skin,** so pulling it hurts.

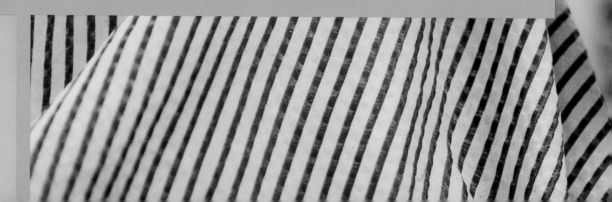

WHY DOESN'T IT HURT TO GET MY HAIR CUT?

Blonds have the **MOST HAIR,** redheads have the least.

Cells are very cool. They are teeny tiny, **almost invisible,** liquid-filled **packs of life.** All living things are made of cells. All living things grow because **cells reproduce them-selves.** Cells make more of you!

A woman in China has **the LONGEST HAIR IN THE WORLD.** It is 18 feet (5.5 meters) long.

HOW DOES HAIR GROW IF IT'S NOT ALIVE?

Hair grows out of the tiny tubes in your skin called **follicles.** Remember the hair you pulled out from your head? On one end is a little bulb.

That's the **root,** where living **cells** come from. As the cells die, they are pushed out of the root, into the follicle, and the hair grows.

29

WHY DO I HAVE TO GO TO BED AT NIGHT?

Scientists are still learning about why people need sleep. In some experiments they make people stay awake. Those people get confused, and angry, and sad. Sleep helps your body take care of itself. You also grow as you sleep.

Your **BRAIN** is making memories while you sleep.

HOW MUCH DO PEOPLE SLEEP?

BABIES
14-17 hours

ONE TO THREE
11-14 hours

THREE TO FIVE
10-13 hours

FIVE TO TWELVE
10-11 hours

TEENAGERS
8-10 hours

WHY DO I HAVE DREAMS AND NIGHTMARES?

It's still a mystery. But scientists know that **when you sleep, your brain is still working.** Everything you touch, see, taste, hear, and smell during the day is tumbled around. So are thoughts, fears, and fun times. Your brain makes mashed-up movies of all these things. Just as with all movies, some are scarier than others.

31

WHY NOT?

You've been learning why people are the way they are. Can you now see why this picture isn't right?

HOW MANY THINGS ARE WRONG IN THIS PICTURE?

Why does
**WATER
FREEZE?**

Why do
**BALLOONS
FLOAT?**

Why do **PLANES FLY?**

2 HOW THINGS WORK

Why does **SOAPY WATER** make bubbles?

WHY DOES WATER TURN TO ICE?

Water turns to ice because it loses heat. Cold air pulls heat out of water. The temperature has to be **32 degrees Fahrenheit** (0 degrees Celsius) to make water begin to freeze.

FROZEN WATER is lighter than liquid water. That's why ice cubes float.

All living things need water. The planet needs water. Do what you can to save water and keep it clean.

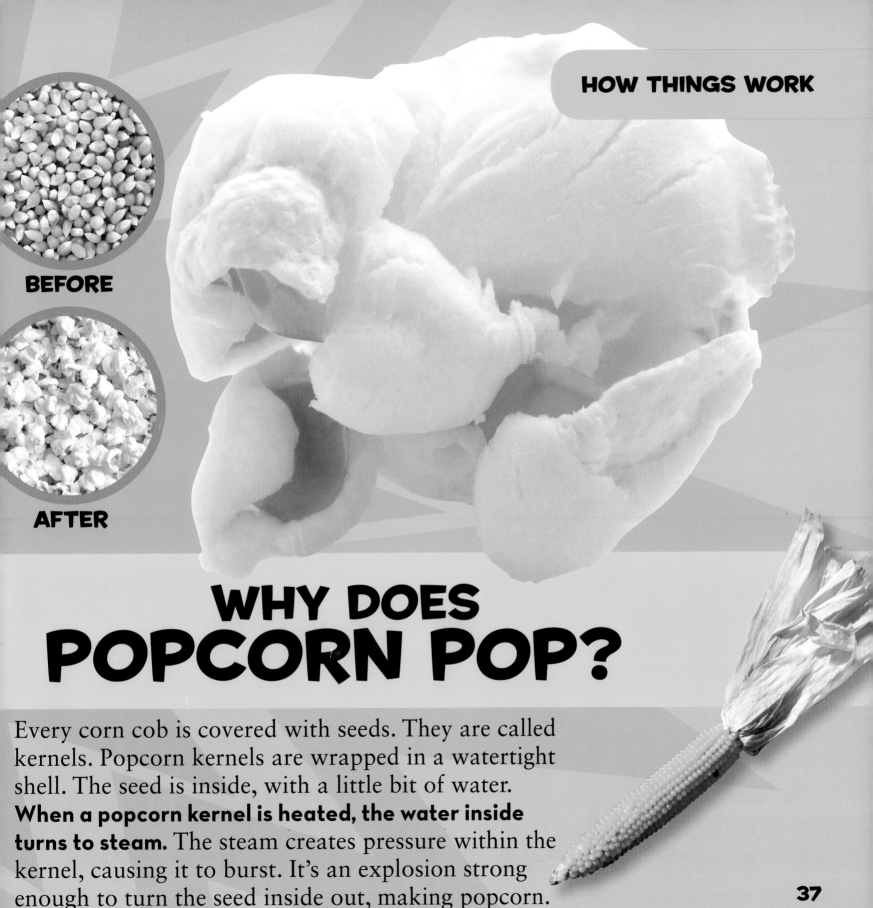

BEFORE

AFTER

WHY DOES POPCORN POP?

Every corn cob is covered with seeds. They are called kernels. Popcorn kernels are wrapped in a watertight shell. The seed is inside, with a little bit of water. **When a popcorn kernel is heated, the water inside turns to steam.** The steam creates pressure within the kernel, causing it to burst. It's an explosion strong enough to turn the seed inside out, making popcorn.

37

They have holes because they cook better without a middle. Plus, it's fun to eat stuff with holes, and bakers want people to like their food.

Holes in **PINEAPPLE** rings are made by people who cut out the tough center of the fruit.

A lot of science happens in the kitchen. When food is changed by cooking or stirring or cooling or heating, science is behind the magic.

Holes in **SWISS CHEESE** are called "eyes."

WHY DO DOUGHNUTS
AND BAGELS HAVE HOLES?

MILK MAGIC EXPERIMENT

Whole milk is mostly just fat and water. When you shake a jar filled with milk, the fat sticks together and leaves some watery milk behind.

YOU'LL NEED

A jar and a pint of heavy cream, room temperature

1 Pour the heavy cream into the jar.

2 Shake until your arms feel like they're going to fall off and then pass the jar to a friend.

3 Keep shaking! After 10 minutes or so, the cream will turn into a solid chunk of butter.

4 Remove butter from jar and divide in half. Blend one half with a little salt. Blend the other half with honey. Taste!

39

WHY DO WE USE A TOILET?

Every animal that eats, poops. Human animals too. People invented toilets so we didn't have to go outside to poop. **How do they work?** When you flush, a big gush of water whooshes into your toilet bowl. All this extra water pushes the waste into a pipe. Then the power of gravity takes the waste out of your house.

WHAT IS GRAVITY?

It pulls everything toward the ground—even your feet! **Without the force of gravity there would be no life on Earth.** Air, water, humans—everything would fly off into space. Gravity is the force within our massive planet Earth that holds our world together.

BEETS make your poop red.

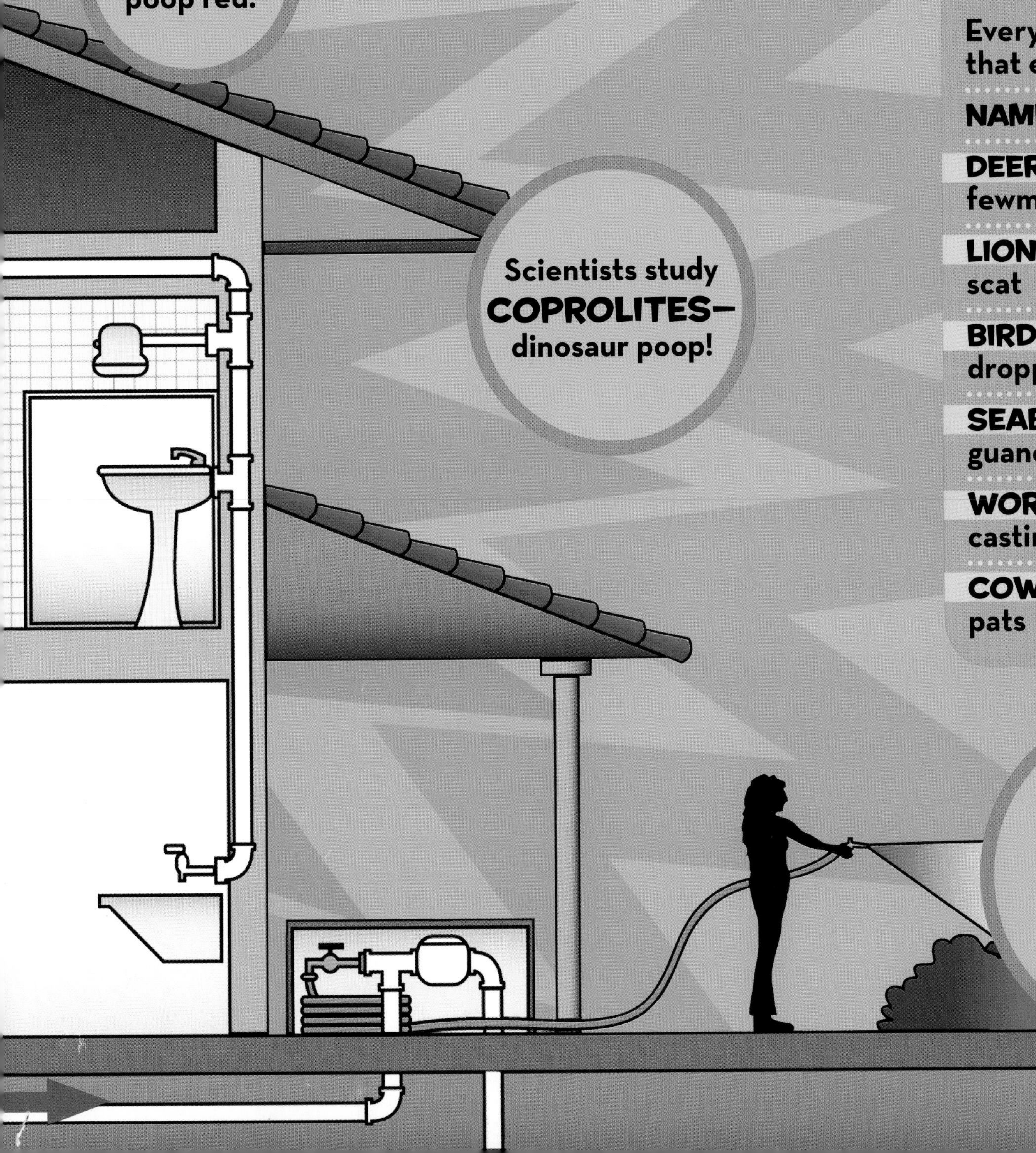

Scientists study **COPROLITES—** dinosaur poop!

FACTS
Every living thing that eats, poops.

NAMES FOR POOP

DEER
fewmets

LION
scat

BIRDS
droppings

SEABIRDS
guano

WORMS
castings

COWS
pats

Solid waste becomes dinner for billions and trillions of **BACTERIA,** who eat it!

41

Bubbles are a thin wrapper of soap filled with air. When air meets soap, the soap sticks together around it. As the air pushes to get out the soap pulls to stay together. This makes a bubble.

WHY DOES SOAPY WATER MAKE BUBBLES?

Next time you're at the aquarium spend some time with the dolphins. They blow air bubbles underwater, and then play with them until they pop.

BUBBLE-ICIOUS EXPERIMENT

Make your own **bubble mix** and experiment with making bubbles.

YOU'LL NEED

2/3 cup dish soap

3 tbsp. glycerine

1 gallon water

1 Mix all the ingredients together. Let sit overnight.

2 Dip your hand in the bubble mix.

3 Curl your fingers to make an O shape and blow!

4 Bubbles want to be round. Can you shape them? What happens to bubbles in the freezer? Try and find out.

WHY DOES A TV WORK?

A TV works because of how our eyes work. First a TV camera takes pictures of actors, about **30 pictures every second.** Each picture is changed into electronic bits of color and brightness. Those electronic bits are sent to a TV transmitter. Some transmitters send the bits by air, some through cables, and some beam them up to satellites in outer space. A TV set captures the bits and turns them back into pictures. On your TV screen, each picture flashes by so fast, one right after another, that **your eyes make them flow together.** Your eyes are tricking you!

The **INVENTOR OF TV,** Philo Farnsworth wouldn't let his kids watch it. He did not think there was anything worth watching.

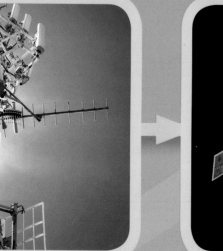

? Do you **WATCH TV?**

WHY DO BALLOONS FLOAT?

Floating balloons are filled with helium. **Helium is a gas that is lighter than air.** Because it is lighter, gravity has less pull on it, and it floats. If you let go of a helium balloon, it could go up for about 6 miles (9.6 km) before it pops.

TRY THIS.

Pour some water into a glass. Then pour in some cooking oil. Oil is lighter than water. It will float on the water. If oil was lighter than air, it would float out of the glass and keep going up.

Hot-air balloons are filled with hot air, heated by propane. Hot air is lighter than cold air, so when the air outside a balloon is colder than the inside, it floats.

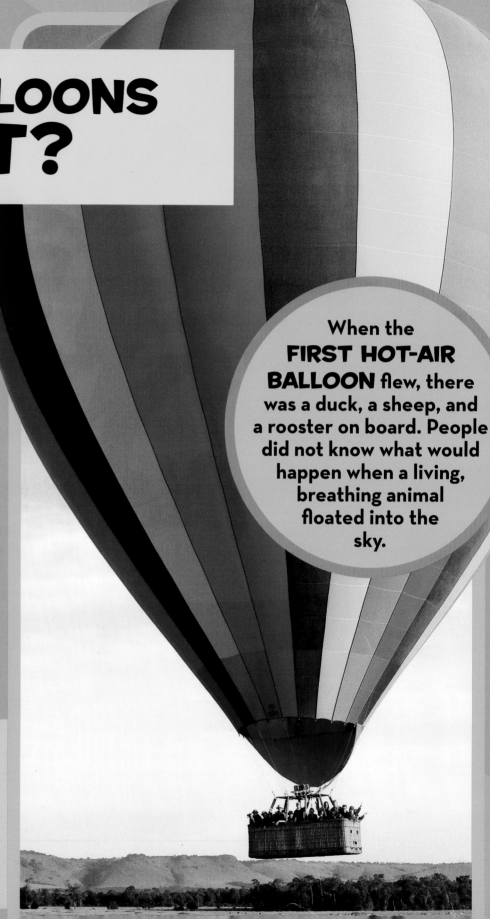

When the **FIRST HOT-AIR BALLOON** flew, there was a duck, a sheep, and a rooster on board. People did not know what would happen when a living, breathing animal floated into the sky.

WHY ARE SOME BUILDINGS SO TALL?

About 130 years ago, some cities had no more land to build upon. There was no room to build bigger. They had to build higher. So up they went, with the help of a new invention—a safe, fast elevator. People called these new buildings skyscrapers.

The highest skyscraper is in **DUBAI**, in the United Arab Emirates. It is 2,717 feet (828 meters) high. It has 163 stories.

Philippe Petit is a high-wire artist. Some wires he walks on go from one skyscraper to another, way up high. Here he is in 1974 walking between the Twin Towers in New York City, 1,368 (417 m) feet in the air.

WHY DOES AN ELEVATOR GO UP AND DOWN?

An elevator carries people up and down in tall buildings.

Imagine a box with a string on top. The string goes up and **over a rolling wheel above.** On the other side of the wheel, the **string is attached to a weight.** The string has to be short so when the weight is on the ground, the box is lifted up. That's the idea of an elevator.

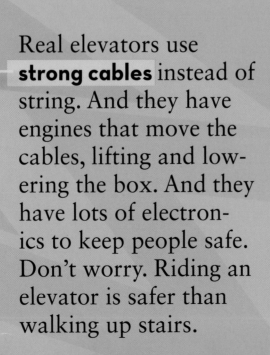

The rolling wheel of an elevator is called a pulley. People invented pulleys thousands of years ago.

Real elevators use **strong cables** instead of string. And they have engines that move the cables, lifting and lowering the box. And they have lots of electronics to keep people safe. Don't worry. Riding an elevator is safer than walking up stairs.

Elevators only go **UP AND DOWN.** There is no side-to-side-elevator, but it is fun to think about!

49

WHY DO THE STAIRS SEEM TO **DISAPPEAR** ON AN **ESCALATOR?**

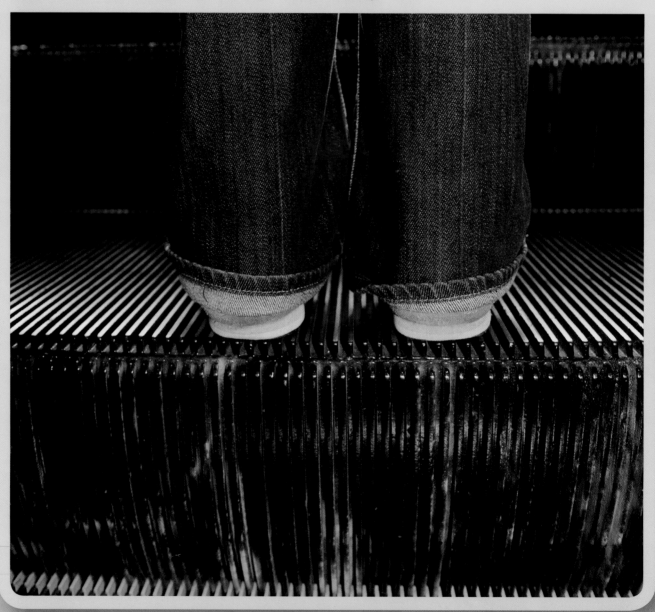

OTHER MOVERS ON LOOPS

Bulldozers

Bike chains

The stairs don't really disappear. The stairs are all hooked together in a loop. After your ride ends at the top, the stairs slide under a metal plate. Then, upside down, they slide back to the bottom. **The loop of stairs goes around and around.**

Roller coasters

? What's the same about these movers? **WHAT'S DIFFERENT?**

Do you think monkeys would like to play on **JUNGLE GYMS?**

The **FIRST PLAY-GROUNDS** had sandboxes, seesaws, swings, and slides.

Another name for jungle gyms is **MONKEY BARS.**

WHY IS A JUNGLE GYM CALLED THAT?

? What do you like to play on the **PLAYGROUND?**

The inventor named these climbing towers jungle gyms. He thought it would be good for kids to be able to play like monkeys do in the jungle. Monkeys have fun hanging, swinging, and climbing. Kids do, too.

WHY DOES AN ICE RINK HAVE A ZAMBONI?

HELLO, ZAMBONI!
It's fun to watch this machine clean the ice for the skaters. **First,** it **shaves** the top of the ice. Then it **scrapes** up the shavings. A warm **wash** of water is sprayed to get every bit of dirt. A **squeegee** scrapes the dirty water into a vacuum. The last step is a **spritz** of hot water. The hot water melts the top of the newly scraped ice. It quickly freezes again, making shiny new ice. All this in 15 minutes!

Ice skaters and hockey players need ice to be as smooth as glass. It is hard to ice skate. It is harder to skate on ice that has cuts and scratches from other skaters.

ROCK CENTER

A **5,000-YEAR-OLD** pair of ice skates were found in Switzerland. They are made of animal bone.

OLYMPIA

A girl in England named Mary Anning was 12 years old when she found **HER FIRST DINOSAUR.**

In 1995 a 14-year-old boy named Wes discovered a birdlike dinosaur. It was named **BAMBIRAPTOR,** after the Disney character Bambi. It is only three feet (91 cm) long.

FACTS

People did not live at the same time as dinosaurs.

Some dinosaurs made nests and laid eggs.

No one knows for sure what sounds dinosaurs made.

Some dinosaurs were more than 100 feet (30.5 meters) long.

Most dinosaurs lived to be more than 100 years old.

WHY ARE DINOSAUR BONES STILL AROUND?

Dinosaurs went extinct, or died out, long ago. But their bones are still being found. **These bones have become fossils.** How do bones become fossils? First the dinosaur had to die in sand or mud, so it would get covered over and preserved. Over a very, very long time the ground became rock, and the bones became fossils.

Jellyfish

Dragonfly

Horseshoe crabs, jellyfish, and dragonflies are some animals that lived with dinosaurs.

Horseshoe crab

WHY CAN I SEE MYSELF IN A MIRROR?

You can see yourself in anything smooth and shiny. Most mirrors are smooth pieces of glass. One side of the glass is painted with a shiny metal. The smooth glass lets light in and the shiny metal bounces it back. Mirrors show you the light from your face. Mirrors do not work in the dark.

Chimpanzees, monkeys, dolphins, and elephants **RECOGNIZE THEMSELVES** in mirrors. Dogs and cats do not.

58

Everyone's eyes are different. Some people need glasses to help their eyes see better. For you to see perfectly, light needs to reach one spot on the back of each eye. If your eye isn't shaped right to focus the light, lenses in glasses can be shaped to focus the light for you.

PUPILS are the part of the eye that let light in. Cats have long, straight pupils. Goats have rectangular pupils.

? **HAVE YOU EVER** looked through someone else's glasses?

WHY DO SOME PEOPLE WEAR GLASSES?

WHY DO PLANES FLY?

Airplanes have really big engines, and that's one thing that helps them fly. But it's really all about air. Try throwing a piece of paper. It doesn't go very far. Fold that paper into an airplane with wings and it will soar. The air works on the wings of your paper airplane just like it does a real plane. The air below the wings pushes up harder than the air flowing over the top of the wing. Hold your hand out the car window sometime and experiment. If your hand is tipped just right it will *vroom* up. **Airplane wings are tipped just right for flying.**

Air works on the wings of a paper airplane just like it does on a real plane.

? **HOW FAR** can your paper airplane fly?

A **747 AIRPLANE** carries about 400 people and weighs almost a million pounds (453 t) at takeoff.

WHY DO BOATS FLOAT?

Boats float because as they push their weight on the water, the water pushes back. **This is called buoyancy.** The shape of a boat also helps the water push back with enough force to hold the boat up. **Next time you go for a swim,** see how your body works in water. If you lie flat on the water, it is easier to float. If you hug your knees and ball up, you will sink.

FLOAT-A-BOAT EXPERIMENT

A flat bottom gives water more to push against. Experiment with different shapes of boats.

YOU'LL NEED

Bowl of water

Play-Doh

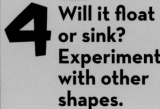

Make a flat-bottom boat shape with a piece of Play-Doh.

2 Place your boat on the water. Does it float?

3 Now make a round ball with a piece of Play-Doh.

4 Will it float or sink? Experiment with other shapes.

WHY NOT?

You've been learning why things work the way they do. Can you now see why this picture isn't right? **HOW MANY THINGS ARE WRONG IN THIS PICTURE?**

Why do **WORMS COME OUT** when it rains?

Why do dogs make **GOOD PETS?**

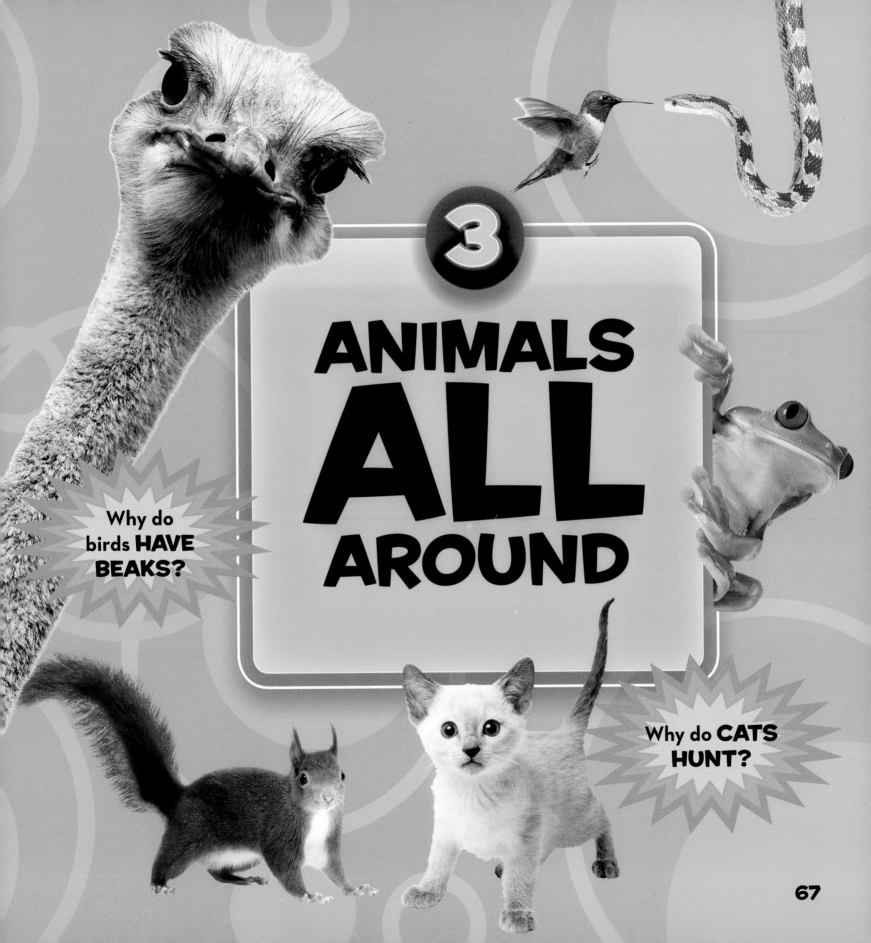

3

ANIMALS ALL AROUND

Why do birds **HAVE BEAKS?**

Why do **CATS HUNT?**

WHY DO DOGS MAKE GOOD PETS?

Dogs are good at listening to people. They know when we are sad or angry. Unlike any other animal, dogs seem to want to make people happy.

Dogs are very nice to pet. PETTING wakes up your sense of touch, unlike just touching something soft.

Dogs have been our helpers for thousands of years. They are the first animals that humans trained and cared for. They are known as "man's best friend."

"I want to be the person **MY DOG THINKS I AM.**"
—bumper sticker

FACTS

Dogs have jobs that help people:

SEEING EYE DOGS help blind people "see" to get around.

POLICE DOGS use their sense of smell to help police fight crime.

SEARCH AND RESCUE DOGS can locate people after storms or earthquakes.

THERAPY DOGS give comfort to people who are not feeling well.

Seeing Eye dogs

Police dogs

Therapy dogs

Search and rescue dogs   **69**

WHY DO CATS HUNT?

At one time all cats were **wild cats.** When people began keeping cats, they wanted them for their hunting skills. **The best hunters kept mice out of houses and barns.** People kept those cats and cared for them. All cats still have a strong instinct to hunt.

Cats are the **MOST POPULAR PET** in the world.

Cats are said to have **9 LIVES.** Why do you think people say this?

FACTS

House cats are still like their wild cousins.

ALL CATS...

...pick up their kittens by the neck to carry them to safety.

...can see in the dark, and have strong senses of smell and hearing.

...have whiskers.

...can twist to land on all four legs if they fall from a height.

...use their tails to balance.

...have tiny hooks on their tongues, making them rough.

WHY DO CATS PURR?

Scientists are not sure why cats purr, but they all do. We think cats purr when they are happy, upset, or don't feel well. That's why scientists think cats purr for lots of reasons. One reason is that purring soothes cats, or makes them feel calm.

Cats also purr when they give birth, perhaps to help the mother cat relax or as a signal to her kittens, who are born blind and deaf. If mother cat is purring, newborns may be able to feel her rumbling and know where she is.

WHY DO WORMS
COME OUT WHEN IT RAINS?

Worms live underground where it is dark and damp. But a big rain brings earthworms out. Maybe this is because it allows them to migrate, or move, to a new location, but scientists aren't sure. Worms breathe through their skin, and they need their skin to be moist to breathe. That's why rainy days may give worms a chance to travel aboveground for a change.

One of the world's largest worms is the **GIANT GIPPSLAND** of Australia. This worm is 3 feet (1 meter) long.

ICEWORMS live in solid ice. If they get too warm they melt.

73

Birds have beaks to eat with, like we have mouths. Do you want to know what they are having for dinner? Look at their beaks to find out.

VULTURES

are meat-eating birds, but they like their meat already dead. Their beaks are not as strong as other meat-eating birds, because they don't have to hunt. They also don't have feathers on their heads. Eating dead meat is messy. A skinhead helps them stay clean.

PELICANS

are scooping fishers. Their lower beak is a pouch. The water they scoop up drains out, leaving the fish behind.

WHY DO BIRDS HAVE BEAKS?

HERONS are stabbing fishers. They spear their dinner with long beaks.

WOODPECKERS are insect-eaters. They have strong, pointed, jabbing beaks for poking holes in wood to uncover insects.

EAGLES are meat-eating birds. They have strong, sharp, hooked beaks for ripping meat.

CARDINALS are seed-eating birds. Their thick, triangle-shaped beaks are like nutcrackers.

HUMMINGBIRDS eat flower nectar. They have long, thin beaks and extendable tongues. The beak of a sword-billed hummingbird is longer than its body.

75

WHY CAN'T FISH BREATHE AIR?

All animals need oxygen to live. Animals that breathe air have lungs that can get oxygen from air. **Fish have gills to get oxygen from water.** Fish gills have to be underwater to work. Gills are feathery, frilly, soft organs that float like waving fingers. Without water, they cannot float. They stick together. They cannot get oxygen.

This salamander has frilly ear-shaped gills on the outside of its body.

Jellyfish do not have gills. They get oxygen **THROUGH THEIR SKIN.**

The walking catfish has special gills. It can breathe in water and on land.

WHY ARE SOME ANIMALS STRIPED?

Tigers are striped.

Tigers are predators. They hunt alone. Their stripes hide them so they can sneak up on prey. They blend in with the grasses where they live. The stalks of grass blur the outline of the tiger.

TIGERS have striped fur and striped skin.

ZEBRAS have black and white stripes.

Zebras live together in herds. Sometimes hundreds of zebras travel together. It is hard for a predator to see just one to chase. **Their stripes make them blur together.**

A zebra's stripes are like your **FINGERPRINTS—** completely unique.

Baby flamingos are gray. They turn pink when they start eating algae. Flamingos that don't eat algae are white.

WHY ARE FLAMINGOS PINK AND ORANGE?

Flamingos get their color from the algae they eat. Algae are plants that live almost everywhere on Earth. The algae flamingos eat have carotene, which colors things orange or pink.

? Can you think of a vegetable that has lots of **CAROTENE?** Hint: It's orange

Animals come in every color you can imagine. Some are many colors at once. Some change color when light shines on them.

Nudibranch

Slug caterpillar

Poison dart frog

Lacewing butterfly

Mandarin duck

Colubrid snake

WHY ARE SOME ANIMALS SO BIG,

There are tiny worms that eat the bones of whales on the bottom of the ocean. One whale skeleton is their entire world.

82

Blue whales have very **DEEP VOICES.** Their sounds travel thousands of miles underwater.

Blue whales weigh up to **200 TONS** (181,000 kg).

Life happens everywhere it can on this amazing planet. **Life comes in every size, shape, and color.** It fills every nook and cranny of the planet. Go outside and look. How many living things can you name?

AND SOME SO SMALL?

There are **TINY CRABS** in Jamaica that spend their whole lives in the puddle of a tree fern.

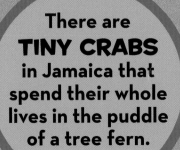

FLEA

TICK

WASP

WHY DO SOME BUGS BITE?

There are millions of bugs in the world. Only a few bite people. Mosquitoes, fleas, bedbugs, and ticks are some that bite. No bugs bite to be mean. Blood is a food they cannot live without. Other bugs bite or sting because they are scared. Some spiders, wasps, bees, and ants will bite or sting if you come too close.

MOSQUITO

Spiderwebs catch spider food. Spiders weave strong webs with sticky spider silk. Small bugs fly or drop in. They cannot pull free. A few strands in the web are not sticky. The spider used these strands to walk on as she built her web. She uses them to travel around it without sticking.

Without spiders, the world would be a buggy place.

WHY DON'T SPIDERS STICK TO THEIR WEBS?

SLOTHS use their strong arms and claws to drag themselves to the next tree.

SLOTHS are the **slowest mammals on Earth**. They live up in a tree, hanging by their hooked claws. Green algae grows on their fur, helping them hide. They eat the leaves of the tree. They are safe from animals that can move a lot faster.

The upside-down Cassiopeia jellyfish needs sunlight on its fringed arms to live.

WHY DO SOME ANIMALS HANG UPSIDE DOWN?

Most animals do what they do to stay safe and get food.

BATS sleep during the day and **hunt for food at night.** The roof of a cave is a safe place for bats to sleep. With their hooked claws, they hang out of reach when other animals are awake and hungry.

Most **BATS** cannot walk. Bats must drop from where they hang to start flying.

These baby opossums are waiting for Mom.

87

WHY DO OWLS THROW UP?

Owls eat mice and other little animals. Whole. In one bite. The leftover bones, fur, and feathers are balled together in an owl's stomach. They throw them up. Scientists call them pellets.

An **OWL PELLET** tells scientists a lot about what owls are eating.

Some **OWLS CAN HEAR** a mouse squeak a half mile (0.8 km) away.

TURKEY VULTURES

throw up when they want predators to go away. Turkey vulture throw-up is really smelly!

COYOTES

throw up food to feed to their young pups before the pups are old enough to hunt.

Horses, beavers, and rats **CANNOT THROW UP.**

WHY DO SNAKES SHED THEIR SKIN?

Snakes grow as they age, but their skin does not grow. When it gets too tight, a snake's skin splits and comes off. Sometimes snakes have to rub themselves on rocks or logs to get it all off. Sometimes it comes off all in one piece.

FACTS

There are about **3,000 DIFFERENT** kinds of snakes in the world.

Most snakes are **NOT POISONOUS** and will not hurt you.

Snakes smell with their **TONGUES.**

Snakes eat their prey **WHOLE.**

Some snakes eat only **ONCE OR TWICE** a year.

Some snakes **LAY EGGS.**

Squirrels **PLAY TRICKS** and only pretend to bury a nut if another squirrel is watching. Then they bury the nut someplace else.

Acorns from red oak trees last a year. Squirrels bury these untouched. Acorns from white oaks will sprout and go bad. Squirrels bite the sprout tip off and often eat the white oak acorns immediately. Squirrels can smell the difference.

WHY DO SQUIRRELS BURY ACORNS?

Many animals prepare for winter. Food is not easy to find in winter. Acorns are in every squirrel's lunch box. They are healthy food and are wrapped in a shell. This makes them a good food to put away. Squirrels spend late summer and early fall collecting acorns and hiding them. They bury them under leaves or tuck them in hollow logs. Squirrels keep a mental map of all their hiding places.

Anyone who likes to feed birds will tell you squirrels are **SUPER SMART!**

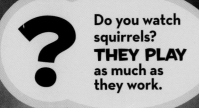

? Do you watch squirrels? **THEY PLAY** as much as they work.

WHY DO COWS MAKE MILK?

Cows are mammals.
They make milk to feed their calves.
Different cows make different kinds
of milk. The milk can be creamier,
94   or a different color.

FACTS

Good grass makes good milk.

Cows need four stomachs to turn grass into milk.

The **1ST STOMACH** mixes the chewed grass with fluid.

The **2ND STOMACH** turns the grass and fluid into little balls. They come back up so the cow can chew some more.

She chews all day long, and passes the mush to the **3RD STOMACH,** which squishes it around.

The **4TH STOMACH** finishes the job.

Honey is winter food for a beehive. During the summer, bees eat nectar and pollen from flowers and plants. They collect nectar in their stomachs as they fly from flower to flower. Back at the hive, other bees chew the nectar. They spread it into beeswax cells called honeycomb. The nectar becomes thick and turns to honey. It is ready for winter.

WHY DO BEES MAKE HONEY?

A bee is the **ONLY INSECT** that makes food eaten by people.

WHY CAN'T WE TALK TO ANIMALS?

We can't talk to animals because we don't know their languages. We know they talk. But they do not use words like we do. They use sounds, and smells, and body language. Bees tell the hive where food and water is by dancing. Bears rub smells on trees to say "Stay away." Kangaroos thump the ground with their tails to warn of danger. Whales sing. Maybe they are singing to communicate with others. Maybe they are trying to attract other whales. Scientists are just not sure.

? Pets are **GOOD LISTENERS.** Do you ever talk to your pet?

WHO'S TALKING EXPERIMENT

2 Get comfortable—you will need to be quiet for a while.

3 Listen to who's talking! Are the birds chirping or screeching? Are the squirrels having fun or yelling at each other?

1 Find a spot away from people sounds like cars and radios.

4 Now close your eyes. You should hear better with your eyes closed.

97

WHY NOT?

You've been learning why animals are the way they are. Can you now see why this picture isn't right? **HOW MANY THINGS ARE WRONG IN THIS PICTURE?**

FIELD TRIP: TH

Why do **SEEDS GROW** up?

WONDERS OF THE WORLD

Why is the **SKY BLUE?**

Why does the **MOON CHANGE** shape?

Why is **SNOW WHITE?**

WHY DO WE SEE A RAINBOW?

What an awesome surprise a rainbow is. Rainbows are sunlight and water. When it has just rained, or is about to rain, there is water in the air. Billions of droplets of water. When sunlight hits the droplets, it separates and we see all the colors of light.

There is an Irish legend that says there is a **POT OF GOLD** at the end of every rainbow.

The **COLORS OF SUNLIGHT** are: red, orange, yellow, green, blue, indigo, and violet.

Next time you're at a waterfall, or a big water fountain, stand with the sun behind you and try to find a rainbow through the water spray.

Light from the sun colors our world. Light can bounce, scatter, bend, or be absorbed, the way a sponge absorbs water. Light is made of the colors of the rainbow. **We see sunlight as white.** So when light bounces, it comes back to us the same color—white. When light is absorbed, it goes away and we see darkness. And we see all different colors when light is scattered.

MAKE-A-RAINBOW EXPERIMENT

You can make a rainbow with water and sunlight.

YOU'LL NEED

A glass filled with water

A piece of white paper

Crayons

1 Place the glass of water on the edge of a windowsill in bright sunlight.

2 Put a piece of white paper on the floor below the glass.

3 Move the glass or your paper until you see the rainbow on the paper.

4 Use crayons to match the rainbow colors on the paper.

WHY IS SNOW WHITE?

Snow is made of air and ice crystals. Snow reflects all colors of light equally. **When they are combined, all the colors look white.** That's why snow looks white.

Black absorbs sunlight. **WEAR BLACK** if you want to stay warm.

Want to **STAY COOL** in summer? Wear white so the sunlight bounces off you.

WHY IS THE SKY BLUE?

The air in the sky has lots of dust and gases like oxygen and ozone. Light from the sun hits these tiny bits and scatters. During the day when the sun is shining bright, the **blue light wave scatters best.** It makes us see the whole sky as blue.

105

WHY DOES THE WIND BLOW?

During the day, the sun heats our planet. **Land heats faster than water.** The air above land is warmed. At night, land loses heat faster than water. The air above land cools. Warm air is lighter than cool air. All this heating and cooling swishes the air around our planet. It is constantly moving. We call that movement wind.

FACTS

Some winds have names.

DIABLO
a strong wind in northern California

ELEPHANTA
a strong wind from the south in India

HABOOB
a fierce dusty wind

HURRICANE
a storm with spiraling winds that begins over the ocean.

WILLY-WILLY
a stormy wind in Australia

Hurricanes are given **BOY AND GIRL NAMES.**

WHY DOES THUNDER COME AFTER LIGHTNING?

Lightning and thunder happen at the same time. **You see the lightning before you hear the thunder** because light travels faster than sound. Have a friend stand way down the sidewalk. Ask her to raise one hand when she sees you clap your hands. Tell her to raise her other hand when she hears the sound of your clap. It will take longer for the sound to reach her ears.

Lightning is formed in thunderclouds. They are called cumulonimbus clouds.

Lightning is a long electrical spark that travels 60,000 miles (96,561 kilometers) per second.

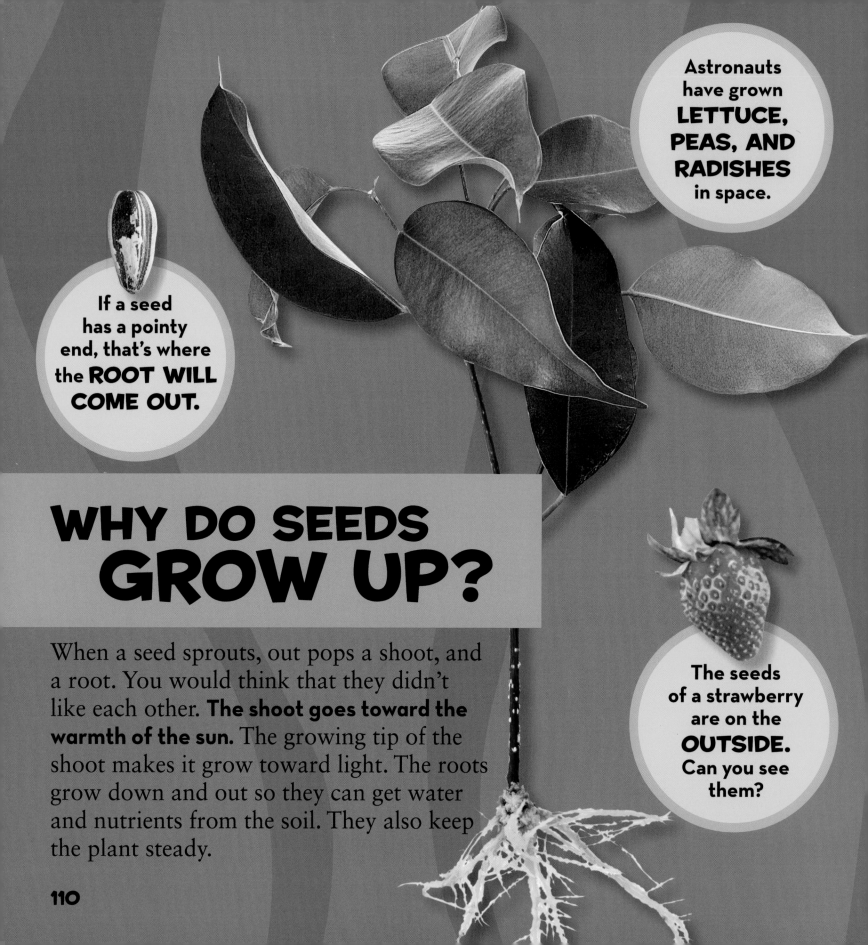

Astronauts have grown **LETTUCE, PEAS, AND RADISHES** in space.

If a seed has a pointy end, that's where the **ROOT WILL COME OUT.**

WHY DO SEEDS GROW UP?

When a seed sprouts, out pops a shoot, and a root. You would think that they didn't like each other. **The shoot goes toward the warmth of the sun.** The growing tip of the shoot makes it grow toward light. The roots grow down and out so they can get water and nutrients from the soil. They also keep the plant steady.

The seeds of a strawberry are on the **OUTSIDE.** Can you see them?

SEED-TO-SPROUT EXPERIMENT

Grow your own plants. If you try this in the summer, you can plant your sprouts outside.

YOU'LL NEED

 Sunflower seeds from a garden store

 Planting pot

 Soil

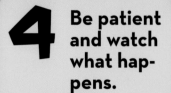

 **1** Put the soil in the pot and poke a shallow hole for each seed.

 **2** Drop one seed in each hole.

 3 Add a little water every other day. Make sure your pot gets plenty of sunlight.

4 Be patient and watch what happens.

WHY IS A BEACH MADE OF SAND?

MOST SAND comes from land, brough to the beach by rivers, streams, rain, and wind.

Sand is plants, rocks, minerals, and seashells worn down to bits by wind and water. A grain of sand on the beach might have been a rock stepped on by a dinosaur. It takes a long time for nature to make sand.

The shells you find on the beach are from soft-bodied animals. They grow shells to protect themselves.

The **BLACK SAND** beaches in Hawaii are made of lava.

Pour some vinegar on sand from the ocean. It will bubble if there are grains of seashells mixed in. Experiment with sand from a stream. Does it bubble?

? Look closely at a handful of sand. Can you see **ROCKS** and **SHELLS?**

What five things would you bring to a **DESERT ISLAND?**

CAYS are islands made of sand or the skeletons of animals called coral.

Greenland is the world's **LARGEST ISLAND.**

WHY DON'T ISLANDS SINK?

Islands don't sink. But they also don't really float. They are surrounded by water, but they are connected to the Earth underwater. Some islands are made by underwater volcanoes. They are connected to the seafloor. Other islands are made when wind and water cut them off from the land.

115

WHY CAN'T WE TOUCH THE STARS?

Stars are too far away to touch. When you see stars in the sky, you are only seeing their light. And that light has traveled a long, long way to get close enough for you to see it. The light from some stars in the sky has been on its way to Earth for many years. **It would take way more than your lifetime to travel to the stars.**

The sun is our closest star. It is **93 MILLION MILES** away.

Stars are born in **STAR NURSERIES.**

Do you ever use your imagination to see the **MAN IN THE MOON?**

We've never seen the **FAR SIDE** of the moon from Earth. We always face the same side.

118

The moon does not have **ITS OWN LIGHT.** It reflects the light of the sun.

WHY DOES THE MOON CHANGE SHAPE?

The moon does not change its shape.
We see only the sunny side of the moon. When we can see the whole sunny side, we call it a full moon. Then the moon begins its trip around Earth. We see less and less of it until it disappears mid-month. Then it comes around the other side of Earth. We see more of it each night until it's a full moon again. It takes a month for the moon to move around the Earth.

119

WHY DON'T WE LIVE ON OTHER PLANETS?

We know why we live on this one. **It's perfect.** People live here on planet Earth because it has **water, air, and food.** Other planets don't have the air, water, and food we need to survive. We have not found another planet like ours, so we had better take care of this one.

Can there be other life in the universe? **Some scientists think there must be life elsewhere.** After all, it's hard to even think about how big the universe is. Is it possible that out of all the galaxies in the universe, only this little planet in one small galaxy supports life? What do you think?

? Maybe someday people will live on other planets, such as Mars. **WOULD YOU LIKE TO LIVE THERE?**

YOU ARE HERE

"The important thing is to **NOT STOP QUESTIONING.**"
—Albert Einstein

WHY NOT?

You've been learning why things in nature are the way they are. Can you now see why this picture isn't right? **HOW MANY THINGS ARE WRONG IN THIS PICTURE?**

122

PARENT TIPS

INHERITANCE
(Observation)
Children are a mix of their parents (p. 15). Other than the traits mentioned in the experiment, look for similarities in body type and facial features. At the next family reunion, have your kids look for similarities and differences among aunts, uncles, cousins, and grandparents.

BUILD A SKYSCRAPER
(Math)
The tallest skyscraper is 2,717 feet (828 meters) high (p. 47). Encourage your child to make a skyscraper from building blocks. Together, count how many blocks you can stack on top of each other before they fall over. Now try building a skyscraper two or more blocks thick. Can you build it higher?

GET STRIPED
(Independence)
Zebras have black and white stripes for protection (p. 79). Have a family zebra day when all of you wear stripes. Take a picture. Do you blend together?

DREAM JOURNAL
(Memory and Imagination)
Dreams are a reflection of everything you touch, see, taste, hear, and smell (p. 31). Each morning, ask your children what he or she dreamed about. Write it down in a journal or let them illustrate their dreams.

WEATHER CHECK
(Measuring Temperature)
Water turns to ice at 32 degrees Fahrenheit (0 degrees Celsius) (p. 36). Using a weather thermometer, help your child measure the temperature of the inside of your house and compare it to the temperature outside, in the freezer, and in the fridge. Talk about hot and cold temperatures inside versus outside, winter versus summer, etc.

TALK ABOUT FOOD
(Nutrition)
Bees are the only insect that make food eaten by people (p. 95). Talk to your child about what foods come from animals (eggs, butter, milk, etc.). Read *Growing Vegetable Soup* by Lois Ehlert.

NO WORDS
(Communication)
We can't talk to animals because we do not know their languages (p. 96). Try communicating with your kids without speaking words. Cut up small pieces of paper and write different words, movie or book titles, actions, or places that all start with the same letter on each scrap. Fold the papers in half and place them in a bowl or hat. One at a time, pick out a word and try to get the other players to guess what it is. You can use sounds, body language, and actions, but no words.

CONCENTRA-TION
(Memory)
The colors of sunlight are red, orange, yellow, green, blue, indigo, and violet (p. 102). Play concentration with a deck of cards you make with your child. Draw simple objects or shapes that match the colors of the rainbow (a red balloon, green apple, yellow star, etc.) on seven index cards. Draw matching pictures on another seven index cards. Then place the shuffled cards facedown on the floor or on a table. Take turns turning over two cards each. If they match, keep them. If they do not match, turn them back over. When all the cards have been matched, count them to see who has collected the most.

MAKE A MOVING PICTURE
(Craft)
On your TV screen, each picture flashes by so fast, one after another, that your eyes make them flow together (p. 44). Direct your own moving picture by making a flip book with your child. Staple 20 Post-it notes or index cards together. Choose an action for your stick figure (running, jumping, swimming, etc). On the first page have your child

raw the stick figure
 starting position.
n each consecutive
age, have your
hild draw the stick
gure in a slightly
ifferent stance so
nat it reaches its final
osition (e.g., land on
ne ground) on the last
age. Flip through the
ook together to see
our picture move!

HOT-AIR BALLOON
(Experiment)

Hot-air balloons are
lled with hot air and
ropane (p. 46). Help
our child explore
he properties of hot
ir by "magically"
nflating a balloon. Fill
 soda bottle with hot
vater and a bowl with
old water. Let both
it for one minute.
mpty the bottle and
tretch a balloon over
he mouth of it. Set
he bottle in the bowl
f cold water and
vatch as the balloon
magically" inflates.

MONKEY AROUND
(Exercise)

he inventor of the
ungle gym thought
 would be good
or kids to play like
nonkeys do in the

jungle (p. 52). Take
a trip with your kids
to a playground.
Encourage them to
climb the monkey bars
like a monkey, run fast
like a cheetah, and
hop like a bullfrog.
Read *Caps for Sale* by
Esphyr Slobodkina.

MIRROR MADNESS
(Playing with Reflections)

Mirrors reflect light
and invert images
(p. 58). Tell your
child to write a
word backward
on a piece of paper
and hold it up to a
mirror. The word
will appear normal
in the mirror! Place
an object between
two parallel mirrors
that face each other.
Change the angle of
the mirrors with your
child to play with the
reflections.

GLOSSARY

ALGAE
a group of plants and plant-like organisms that usually grow in water

BACTERIA
single-celled micro-organisms that live inside every living thing

CAYS
islands made of sand or the skeletons of coral piled and crushed together over time

CELL
the teeny tiny basic unit of which every living thing is composed

FOLLICLE
a tiny, thin tube in your skin through which each strand of hair grows

GALAXY
a part of the universe that contains a system of stars and interstellar matter. Earth is in the Milky Way galaxy.

GILLS
body organs that allow fish and other organisms to get oxygen underwater

MAMMALS
a group of animals, including humans, that are warm-blooded, breathe air, have hair, and nurse their young

MELANIN
a pigment that darkens skin and protects it from the sun

OMNIVORE
an animal that eats meat and plants

PELLET
a ball of indigestible material, including bones and fur, thrown up by birds of prey

ROOT
the living part at the beginning of each hair follicle; also a part of plants

ADDITIONAL RESOURCES

BOOKS

Hughes, Catherine D. *Little Kids First Big Book of Animals.* Washington, D.C.: National Geographic Children's Books, 2010.

Laffron, Martine. *The Book of Why.* Abrams, 2006.

Ripley, Catherine. *Why?: The Best Ever Question and Answer Book about Nature, Science and the World Around You.* Toronto: Owlkids, 2010.

TIME for Kids BIG Book of Why: 1,001 Facts Kids Want to Know. New York: Time for Kids, 2010.

Weird but True! Washington, D.C.: National Geographic Children's Books, 2009.

WEBSITES

kids.nationalgeographic.com

pbskids.org

kidrex.org

sciencekids.co.nz/experiments.html

kids-science-experiments.com

teacherstryscience.org/parents/se_1.html

INDEX

Boldface indicates illustrations.

A
Acorns **92,** 93
Aging 18, **18**
Airplanes 60, **60–61,** 61
Anning, Mary 56

B
Bacteria 23, 41
Bagels 38
Balloons 46, **46**
Bambiraptor 56
Bats 87, **87**
Beaches 112–113, **112–113**
Bears 96, **96**
Beavers 22, **22,** 89
Bees 84, 95, **95,** 96
Beets 41
Belly buttons 12–13, **12–13**
Bike chains **51**
Birds 41, **74,** 74–75, **75**
Blue whales 82, **82–83,** 83
Boats 62, **62,** 63
Brain 30, 31
Breathing 73, 76
Bubbles 42, **42,** 43, **43**
Bugs 84, **84**
Buildings 47, **47,** 48–49, **48–49**
Bulldozers **51**
Butter 39
Butterfly **81**

C
Cameras, TV 44
Candy 25, **25**
Cardinals 75, **75**
Carrots 24, **24**
Cassiopeia jellyfish 86, 8
Caterpillar **81**
Cats 13, **13,** 58–59, **59, 70,** 70–71, **71**
Cays (islands) 115, **115**
Cells 29
Chimpanzees 13, **13,** 58
Clouds 108, **108**
Colors
   of animals 80–81
   to keep you cool 105
   to keep you warm 104
   of skin 10–11, **10–11**
   of the sky 104
   of snow 104
   of sunlight 102
Colubrid snake **81**
Communication by animals 96–97
Coprolites 41
Corals and coral reefs 115 **115**
Cows 41, 94, **94**
Coyotes 89, **89**
Crabs 83
Crocodiles 23, **23**

D
Dinosaurs 41, 56, **56–57,** 5
Doctors 20, **20**
Dogs 13, **13,** 19, **19,** 58, **68,** 68–69, **69, 96**
Dolphins 13, **13,** 42, **42,** 58
Doughnuts 38, **38**
Dragonflies **57**
Dreams 31
Dubai, United Arab Emirates 47, **47**
Duck **81**

FOR EVERYONE WHO KEEPS ASKING WHY—AND WHY NOT! —AS

Prepared by the Book Division
Nancy Laties Feresten, Senior Vice President, Editor in Chief,
  Children's Books
Jonathan Halling, Design Director, Children's Publishing
Jennifer Emmett, Editorial Director, Children's Books
Carl Mehler, Director of Maps
R. Gary Colbert, Production Director
Jennifer A. Thornton, Managing Editor

Staff for This Book
Jennifer Emmett, Project Editor
Eva Absher, Art Director
Lori Epstein, Senior Illustrations Editor
Annette Kiesow, Illustrations Editor
Erin Mayes, Designer, EmDash Design
Kate Olesin, Editorial Assistant
Hillary Moloney, Illustrations Assistant
Raina Davis, Editorial Intern
Grace Hill, Associate Managing Editor
Lewis R. Bassford, Production Manager
Susan Borke, Legal and Business Affairs

Manufacturing and Quality Management
Christopher A. Liedel, Chief Financial Officer
Phillip L. Schlosser, Senior Vice President
Chris Brown, Technical Director
Nicole Elliott, Manager
Rachel Faulise, Manager
Robert L. Barr, Manager

Since 1888, the National Geographic Society
has funded more than 12,000 research,
exploration, and preservation projects around
the world. The Society receives funds from
National Geographic Partners, LLC, funded in
part by your purchase. A portion of the proceeds
from this book supports this vital work. To learn
more, visit www.natgeo.com/info.

NATIONAL GEOGRAPHIC and Yellow Border
Design are trademarks of the National Geographic
Society, used under license.

For more information, please call 1-800-647-5463
or write to the following address:
National Geographic Partners, LLC
1145 17th Street N.W.
Washington, D.C. 20036-4688 U.S.A.

Visit us online at www.nationalgeographic.com/
books

For librarians and teachers:
www.ngchildrensbooks.org

More for kids from National Geographic:
natgeokids.com

For information about special discounts for bulk
purchases, please contact National Geographic
Books Special Sales: specialsales@natgeo.com

For rights or permissions inquiries, please contact
National Geographic Books Subsidiary Rights:
bookrights@natgeo.com

The Library of Congress has cataloged the original
editions as follows:

Shields, Amy, author.
  Little kids first big book of why / By Amy Shields.
   p. cm
  Includes index.
  ISBN 978-1-4263-0793-5 (hardcover : alk. paper) --
  ISBN 978-1-4263-0792-8 (library binding : alk. paper)
  1. Children's questions and answers. I. Title.
AG195.S46 2011
031.02--dc22
                                          2010043147

Printed in the United States of America

17/LSCK-PCML/13 (Trade)
17/LSCK-PCML/3 (RLB)

Special thanks to educational consultant
Dr. Alice Wilder, *Blue's Clues, Super Why,* Think It Ink It Publishing Kidos

GET: Getty Images
IS: iStockphoto
NGS: NationalGeographicStock.com
SS: Shutterstock

COVER: Clockwise from top left, © Bill Heinsohn/ Photographer's Choice/ GET; © Morgan Lane Photography/ SS; © Frances A. Miller/ SS; © Vibrant Image Studio/ SS; © Chris Leachman/ SS; © Barry Willis/ Photographer's Choice/ GET; © Olga Bogatyrenko/ SS; © FikMik/ SS; © IKO/ SS.

BACK COVER: (top, right), Lucie Lang/ SS; (bottom, right), Utekhina Anna/ SS; SPINE, Vishnevskiy Vasily/ SS; 2 (top, left), © GK Hart/ Vikki Hart/ The Image Bank/ GET; 2 (bottom, left), © Jeremy Richards/ SS; 2 (center), © Andreas Kermann/ IS; 2 (right), © Tom Vezo/ Minden Pictures/ NGS; 3 (top), © Ricksku/ SS; 3 (right), © Lucky Keeper/ SS; 3 (bottom), © S. Wanke/ Photolink/ GET; 4, © Jon Beard/ SS.

Amazing Me:
6 (left), © Yuri Arcurs/ SS; 6 (center), © Yalayama/ SS; 6 (right), © Yuri Arcurs/ SS; 7 (left), © Dmitriy Shironosov/ SS; 7 (right), © Ana Abejon/ IS; 8, © Jaimie Duplass/ SS; 9 (top, left), © Miodrag Gajic/ IS; 9 (top, right), © Prill Mediendesign & Fotografie/ IS; 9 (bottom), © Lori Epstein/ www.loriepstein.com; 10, © Tom Grill/ Corbis/ SS; 11, © Marilyn Barbone/ SS; 12, © Mike Kemp/ Rubberball; 13 (top and inset), © Jeff Rotman Photography; 13 (bottom, left), © Muriel Hazan/ Photolibrary; 13 (center), © ZTS/ SS; 13 (bottom, right), © Ian Nichols/ NGS; 14 (right), © Caroline Purser/ Photographer's Choice/ GET; 15, © Lori Epstein/ www.loriepstein.com; 15 (left, inset), © RMAX/ IS; 15 (bottom), © Lori Epstein/ www.loriepstein.com; 17, © Barry Willis/ Photographer's Choice/ GET; 18, © Ryan McVay/ Photodisc/ GET; 19 (left), © Don Johnston/ Alamy; 19 (right), © Festus Robert/ SS; 20 (top), © Dorling Kindersley/ GET; 20 (bottom), © GeoM/ SS; 21 (all), © Lori Epstein/ www.loriepstein.com; 22 (left) from top to bottom, © Paul Nicklen/ NGS; © Anke van Wyk/ SS; © Kurt Madersbacher/ Photolibrary; Nature's Images/ Photo Researchers, Inc.; 22 (right), © Gary John Norman/ The Image Bank/ GET; 23 (top), © Thomas M. Perkins/ SS; 23 (bottom), © Anan Kaewkhammul/ SS; 24 (inset), © chungking/ SS; 24, © Morgan Lane Photography/ SS; 25, © Lucie Lang/ SS; 25 (inset), © Stephen Aaron Rees/ SS; 26, © Chris Leachman/ SS; 27 (top), © Huntstock/ SS; 27 (bottom), © ifong/ SS; 27 (right), © Christi Tolbert/ SS; 28, © rickt/ SS; 29, © Karina Bakalyan/ SS; 30 (left), © Handy Widiyanto/ SS; 30 (right), © DNF-Style Photography/ SS; 31, © Catmando/ SS; 32-33, photo illustration by Eva Absher, all photos from © SS except: girl playing frisbee, girl singing, and basketball, © IS.

How Things Work:
34 (left), © Bill Heinsohn/ Photographer's Choice/ GET; 34 (right), © Kotenko Oleksandr/ SS; 35 (top), © Stephen Strathdee/ IS; 35 (bottom), © kotomiti/ SS; 36 (left), © Na Gen Imaging/ Workbook Stock/ GET; 36 (right), © Don Nicols/ IS; 37 (top, left), © Tom Grundy/ SS; 37 (bottom, left), © Glock/ SS; 37 (center), © Jan Martin Will/ SS; 37 (bottom, right), © Joe Potato Photo/ IS; 38, © Chris Leachman/ SS; 39 (top, left), © mm88/ IS; 39 (top, center), © Joe Potato Photo/ SS; 39 (t), © CostinT/ IS; 39 (top right, and 2, 3, 4), © Lori Epstein/ www.loriepstein. com; 40-41, © Luis Carlos Torres/ IS; 42 (left), © Fco Javier Gutierrez/ age fotostock/ Photolibrary; 42 (right), © Frances A. Miller/ SS; 43 (all), © Mark Thiessen/ NGS; 44 (top), © Feng Yu/ SS; 44 (bottom, left), © Sinisa Botas/ SS; 44 (bottom, right), © Cico/ SS; 45 (top), © Palto/ SS; 45 (top, inset), © Nick Biemans/ SS; 45 (bottom, left), © Manfred Steinbach/ SS; 45 (bottom, right), © Cheryl Casey/ SS; 46, © Michael Poliza/ NGS; 47 (left), © KENCKOphotography/ SS; 47 (right), © AP Photo/ Alan Welner; 48, © imagebroker/ Alamy; 49 (left), © Steven Haggard/ Alamy; 49 (right), © Astock/ Corbis; 50, © Lori Epstein/ www.loriepstein.com; 51 (top, left), © Minisrt-84/ SS; 51 (bottom, left), © WilleeCole/ SS; 51 (center), © Dmitry Kalinovsky/ SS; 51 (bottom, right), © Brett Mulcahy/ SS; 52, © John Burcham/ NGS; 54, © zoommer/ IS; 55, © Stephane Hubert/ Digital Light Source/ Photolibrary; 56, © Lowell Georgia/ NGS; 57 (top), © Mircea Bezergheanu/ SS; 57 (bottom), © Edgewater Media/ SS; 57 (right), © Ivan Cholakov Gostock-dot-net/ SS; 58, © Jupiterimages/ Comstock Images/ GET; 59 (left), © IKO/ SS; 59 (top, right), © Brenda Carson/ SS; 59 (center, right), © Jag_cz/ SS; 60 (inset), © Denis and Yulia Pogostins/ SS; 60-61, © Vibrant Image Studio/ SS; 62, © Stringer/ Reuters/ Corbis; 63 (all), © Mark Thiessen/ NGS; 64-65, photo illustration by Eva Absher, all photos from © SS except: checker board, dinosaur, and cows, © IS.

Animals All Around:
66 (top, left), © Volodymry Krasyuk/ SS; 66 (center, left), © Mikhail Melnikov/ SS; 66 (bottom, left), © Susan Schmitz/ SS; 66 (top, center), © Milos Luzanin/ SS; 66 (center), © Eric Isselée/ SS; 66 (top, right), © Eric Isselée/ SS; 67 clockwise from top left, © Vishnevskiy Vasily/ SS; © Steve Byland/ SS; © B. Stefanov/ SS; © FikMik/ SS; © Utekhina Anna/ SS; © Eric Isselée/ SS; © Sergey Lavrentev/ SS; 69 (left), © iofoto/ SS; 69 (top, right), © Lars Christensen/ SS; 69 (center, right), © Jan Tyler/ IS; 69 (bottom, right), © Jim Parkin/ SS; 70 (both), © Konrad Wothe/ Minden Pictures/ NGS; 71, © Orhan Cam/ SS; 72, © Don Paulson/ Alamy; 73 (top), © mashe/ SS; 73 (bottom, left), © Accent Alaska.com/ Alamy; 73 (bottom, right), © John O'Neil/ ANTPhoto.com.au; 74 (left), © Kay Neitfeld/ dpa/ Corbis; 74 (right), © Mogens Trolle/ SS; 75 (top, left), © Dirk Freder/ IS; 75 (top, right), © FloridaStock/ SS; 75 (bottom, left), © Ronnie Howard/ SS; 75 (bottom, center), © Chris Alcock/ SS; 75 (bottom, right), © iDesign/ SS; 76, © Bruce Coleman Inc./ Alamy; 76-77, © Specta/ SS; 77 (inset), © Robert Sisson/ NGS; 78, © Theo Allofs/ Photonica/ GET; 79, © Eric Isselée/ SS; 80 (left), © Tom Vezo/ Minden Pictures/ NGS; 80 (right), © Windzepher/ IS; 81 (top), © Luiz A. Rocha/ SS; 81 (center, left), © Mark Moffett/ Minden Pictures/ NGS; 81 (center), © Sascha Gebhardt/ IS.com; 81 (center, right), © James Laurie/ SS; 81 (bottom, left), © Michal Potok/ SS; 81 (bottom, right), © Mark Moffett/ Minden Pictures/ NGS; 82 (inset), © Darlyne A. Murawski/ NGS; 82-83, © Denis Scott/ Corbis; 83, clear-viewstock/ SS; 84 (left), © D. Kucharski & K. Kucharski/ SS; 84 (top), © Daniel Cooper/ IS; 84 (center, right), © irin-k/ SS; 84 (bottom), © Henrik Larsson/ SS; 85, © Mirvav/ SS; 86 (top), © Eric Isselée/ SS; 86 (inset), © Norbert Wu/ Minden Pictures/ NGS; 87 (top), © John Carnemolla/ SS; 87 (bottom), © Frank Lukasseck/ Corbis; 88 (inset), © Konrad Wothe/ Minden Pictures/ NGS; 88, © Scott Linstead/ FN/ Minden Pictures/ NGS; 89 (left), © Denis Pepin/ SS; 89 (right), © Enrique R. Aguirre Aves/ Alamy; 90, © Heidi and Hans-Jurgen Koch/ Minden Pictures/ NGS; 91 (top), © Alan Weaving/ Ardea.com; 91 (bottom), © Paul Tessier/ IS; 92 (inset), © Martin Shields/ Alamy; 92, © Andrew Darrington/ Alamy; 93, © Jay Shrestha; 94, © Christopher Elwell/ SS; 95 (left), © LilKar/ SS; 95 (right), © Michael Avory/ SS; 96 (left), © Ariel Skelley/ The Image Bank/ GET; 96 (right), © Giel/ Taxi/ GET; 97, © Radius Images/ Corbis; 97 (top, inset), © Maksym Gorpenyuk/ SS; 97 (top, right), © irin-k/ SS; 97 (right, inset), © Bruce MacQueen; 98-99, photo illustration by Eva Absher, all photos from © SS except basketball, © IS.

Wonders of the World:
100 (left), © Tobias Helbig/ IS; 100 (right), © Dmitry Kosterev/ SS; 101 (left), © pakowacz/ SS; 101 (right), © Yaroslav/ SS; 102, © Jeremy Richards/ SS; 103 (all), © Mark Thiessen/ NGS; 104, © Losevsky Pavel/ SS; 105, © Pakhnyushcha/ SS; 106, © Gorilla/ SS; 107 (top), © Alistair Berg/ Digital Vision/ GET; 107 (bottom), © NASA/ JSC/ ES&IA; 108, © Nicolas McComber/ SS; 109, © Marco Alegria/ SS; 110 (left), © F.C.G./ SS; 110 (center), © Beata Becia/ SS; 110 (right), © szefei/ SS; 111 (all), © Becky Hale/ NGS; 112, © Yory Frenklakh/ IS; 113 (top, left), © Nyvlt-art/ SS; 113 (top, right), © USGS/ HVO; 113 (bottom), © Darren Greer/ SS; 114, © Nickolay Stanev/ SS; 115, © Peter Harrison/ Ticket/ Photolibrary; 116, © NASA/ JPL; 117, © Christophe Lehenaff/ Photononstop/ Photolibrary; 118, © ravi/ SS; 119, © Gwoeii/ SS; 120-121, © NASA/ JPL; 121 (inset), © NASA/ HQ/ GRIN; 122-123, photo illustration by Eva Absher, all photos from © SS except Saturn, © NASA STI; tornado, © Don Farrall/ Photodisc/ GET; woman on ladder, snowflakes, periscope, roses, and © snowglobe, © IS.